Coast
Mountain
Foot

Also by

ryan fitzpatrick

Poetry
Fake Math
*Fortified Castles**

Editor
Why Poetry Sucks: An Anthology of Humorous
Experimental Canadian Poetry
(with Jonathan Ball)

* Published by Talonbooks

Coast
Mountain
Foot

Poems

ryan fitzpatrick

Talonbooks

Talonbooks
9259 Shaughnessy Street, Vancouver, British Columbia, Canada V6P 6R4
talonbooks.com

Talonbooks is located on xʷməθkʷəy̓əm, Sḵwx̱wú7mesh, and səlilwətaʔɬ Lands.

First printing: 2021

Typeset in Minion
Printed and bound in Canada on 100% post-consumer recycled paper

Interior and cover design by Typesmith
Cover photograph: *Overcast* by Edna Winti via Flickr.com (CC BY 2.0)

Talonbooks acknowledges the financial support of the Canada Council for the Arts, the Government of Canada through the Canada Book Fund, and the Province of British Columbia through the British Columbia Arts Council and the Book Publishing Tax Credit.

Library and Archives Canada Cataloguing in Publication

Title: Coast Mountain foot : poems / Ryan Fitzpatrick.
Names: Fitzpatrick, Ryan, 1978– author.
Identifiers: Canadiana 20210138211 | ISBN 9781772013597 (softcover)
Classification: LCC PS8611.I893 C63 2021 | DDC C811/.6—dc23

Today I wake up with the
sound of Vancouver
energy in my ears.
The streets running wide
& shiny to the beaches
filled with poets & movie-men
hippies in convertibles,
slant under my shoes of
prairie dust.

　　　　–George Bowering
　　　　　Rocky Mountain Foot
　　　　　(1968)

I think that in the new society
we'll let people be unhappy if they want.

—Helen Potrebenko
Walking Slow
(1985)

COAST MOUNTAIN FOOT

Does
the sun
come up?

It's only
a property
question.

Selfie
any
street.

Develop
any
corner.

"Over and
Over" heard
overhead.

Air
space
thick.

By thick,
I mean
dense.

By dense,
I mean
tall.

Still cash,
even local,
sloughs.

Pools at
cloud
height.

MORE LIKE COASTING THROUGH

Today I wake
to the sound
of energy –

the energy
in these
streets.

A shitty
metaphor
for relation

in a city
where your
job's likely oil.

Walk over
to the turntable
(or the computer),

turn over that
copy of *Rocky
Mountain High* –

from "Season
Suite" to
the title track

and its hippie
obsession with
natural spirituality.

What decade
is it today,
what century?

What city does
a poem write
when the city

tips itself over,
turned back
to the A-side?

VANCOUVER DOES NOT TASTE LIKE CALGARY

How to start
writing about
any city?

Is it anything
like living
somewhere

when you
don't feel
so welcome?

A shitty question
when structures
benefit you

though they
never feel
too beneficial

when rent
is cheaper inside
the couple form

or when work
involves constantly
bootstrapping

all the slack
anxiety of
comfortable precarity.

What does
that ad say
across the street?

Pocketed deep
inside the doors
at Hastings and Howe.

"Luxury never
makes anyone
beautiful."

They're debating
view cones
at the edge

of the
upcoming
civic election,

whether seeing
the mountains
is an amenity

if the developers
near the stadium
keep their word

about building
1,800 units
of social housing,

unlike the
rug-pull
of Olympic Village

where they
felt the
sudden luxury

of all that
prime waterfront
real estate

unlocking like
the tides
through Sen̓áḵw/sən̓aʔqʷ

were gulped
by Vancouver's
swallowing growth.

Managing
Vancouver's
postcard view

is a hell
of a tough
question

when you
scoff at
privileging sightlines,

but also
love that view
down Main

even if
it raises
property values.

Some places
you can only
see mountains

hitting the crest
at Glenmore
and Blackfoot.

YET ANOTHER LONG POEM
ABOUT VANCOUVER

Can I live in
Vancouver without
writing about it?

All that work
done better in
the last century

even if the
freeway traffic
is still moving.

Sand grits
against the slick
leaves of my walk

as another umbrella's
broken line
sings its rainfall

through Marlatt's
Steveston vs. Parks
Canada's Steveston,

Potrebenko's West
End vs. Amy and
Sean's West End.

Where do I find
Kiyooka's pear tree
($50 at Paper Hound)

or my $746/month
apartment where
I can palm the ceiling?

Friendly egalitarianism.
Self-elected liberal. "The excellence
and energy sportsmanship requires."
Power intimacy. Abstract assertion.
"Limited to the living." Claiming title.
"The nation claims the burden of
trauma for itself." Critique foreclosure.
"A cultural response to a political
challenge." Rubble as hand of god.
Therapeutic commune. "What will the
city look like to me afterward?" This
insecure future. This terminal empathy.
"One waits for permission to go on."
Violated code. Gated distinction.

06/23/12

LORD, I'M SET TO CRY

On an apartment,
a sign won't say vacancy.

Renoflection evinces
a square-footaged fang.

A blanket-slow repayment
tenets vacate.

So happy alone,
dishwashing.

An over-certain root
chinooks.

Numbers hook
number to number.

Like any ice floe,
tankers shore alarm.

Basement cost index
sunsets cornea.

Paper surely conquers
inflationary value.

Novict swell lumbers
nail into hammer.

Landlord ships
fail state climate.

Sophisticate tenants
out for blood.

Utility bill
tears up bathroom.

Swelled dial rolls
up cuffed affect.

So welled up,
maybe it'll rain?

Offloading austerity. New
relationships. Our structural adjustments.
Other ways of struggle. Lectureship. "Recreating
militant research." Active principle. A
past dripped out. Underground current.
Overflows and cracks. Power as potencia.
A taste for the case. Organizational
experiment. 2001 is everywhere. A
way out of neoliberalism. Politicizing
sadness. Co-optation vs. heroic marginalization.
Social policy to sustain consumption. Our
fate's multiple contradictions. A way out
of the state's indelible essence. Politics
in two faces. From rights to financialization.
Trace copy. "They weren't just making
demands." Political disorientation. No
solutions, only problematizations. Neo-
extractivist. Empathy verification.

11/13/12

IT LIVENS UP A DEAD SPACE

The present
is a gift

across buildings
and beer labels.

Building condemned,
except for artists.

Development budget
as practised ruin.

Only a
seafood market,

only a
decommissioned school,

only an
evicted block,

only a
renovicted floor.

Leases signed
under duress.

Our place,
our home.

"... the building
landlord blocked

the muralists
from using

portraits of two
Belvedere residents ..."

Slated for
eventual demolition,

shipping containers as
retail space,

No wall
left unmuralled.

Love in the
time of parking.

More New
Urbanist horseshit

about the form
of the city.

JUST A QUICK SNAPSHOT

If it's a ruin,
what about it
has changed?

Another tag
lights another
concrete texture.

Sunset anchored
over English
Bay tankers.

Some yacht rock
real estate
finance capital.

The frictionless
squeeze of "What
a Fool Believes."

How many hours
have I lost
this week

trying hard to
recreate what
had yet to be?

The neighbouring
penthouse lights
on a timer

keeping rhythm
for the logistics
passing through.

EVERYTHING I TOOK
I'D SOON RETURN

A few hundred
snapshots out of
café windows.

A few hundred
from inside the
bus shelter.

That vernacular
catch for weather
out of step.

Like snow, so
hard to get
on film,

unless I
stretch time into
a short gif.

It's social –
whether the
sun comes up.

How hot
it sits on
my back.

What was it
that Kristeva
said?

Something about
the street lamps
along Morley Trail

or the trees along
Main Street
in April?

Distributive
vulnerability. "I felt a little bit
indignant." Transmission breaks.
Foundational period. "One willing to
represent." "Faith needs more than
style." This inconsistent grammar.
Simple sneer. "Proper names + font sizes."
Alienation by digital effect. Important
work. Salvaging apology. Preserving
the authentic contaminated. "What
happens when you give up?"

05/28/12

THE ECONOMIC CASE FOR
TACKLING LONELINESS

What is
the mode
of writing

best suited
to mapping
the social?

I used
to think
about recombination,

which is
really the kind
of appropriation

where you
turn the oil
into Cool Whip.

How many cars
have passed by
in the last minute?

How many
stopped at
the stop sign?

How much gas
burned idling
in the cold?

What's in
their tape deck,
iPhone, etc.?

Who was it
spit against
this window?

How many days
to wait until
you complain

about a shipment
that hasn't
arrived yet?

That book
I've been
waiting for –

how many
hands has it
passed through?

That's a pretty
silly question
to ask

about global
logistics as they
play intimately.

When Laura
sings, "Oh
my dear,

it's only
love that
keeps us here,"

I want
so badly
to believe it,

but it's hard
when the
city form

can't imagine
life outside
sex and work.

Shit, in my
most cynical
moments,

what is here
if not structure
on the move?

What would
Marx say
about that?

Something about
capitalist totality
holding us together.

After all,
emergence doesn't
feel like much

in the belly
of development
gone wild.

But also,
it's just hard
to ask someone,

"Hey, do you
want to
imagine

new forms
of social
intimacy"

without it
coming off as
a pickup line.

AND TOMORROW,
I'M SOMEONE ELSE

Remember the
Calgary Tower
as the tallest building

when it was
named after
Husky Energy,

replaced by the
Petro-Can towers
on 5th, renamed

the Suncor
Energy Centre,
then The Bow

planned by Encana,
then sold to
an investment trust

who completed
the project
in 2012, though

they didn't build
that second tower,
did they?

Two public
artworks
on the site,

required by
city regulations
trading in density,

a giant head
(*Wonderland* by
Jaume Plensa),

and "The Tree
Hugger" (*Alberta's
Dream* – also Plensa).

Memory sometimes
just a fantasy
of who we are.

Robert Bateman
too political
for city hall,

but when does
George Vancouver's
statue come down?

He stands
on the steps
of city hall,

looking like
he discovered
something.

YOU CAN'T JUST TAKE A NAME

How many
elbows does
a city need?

The position
jockeying of
freeway living

a way to
beat back
throttling bottlenecks.

A history that
paves over
its history

as if memory
were a form
of texture.

The excessive
highway speed
of Deerfoot Trail

a strange tribute
to the famed
Siksiká runner.

Sarcee Trail
only turns
into Tsuut'ina Trail

mediated by
a messy interchange
with Glenmore.

The Kainai
absent from
the road map

because officials
didn't want a
Blood Trail.

Speeding toward
the horizon line
on Highway 2,

imagine entering
the city,
welcomed to

Mohkínstsis,
Wichispa Oyade,
Guts'ists'i,

and left wondering
if Vancouver's
street names

stayed so colonial
because they didn't
finish the freeway.

THE ENERGY IN THESE STREETS

On the 3,
a conversation
about the driver

and Vancouver's
sometimes aggressive
unfriendliness

turns to one
about the
Calgary election.

Nenshi wins
in a squeaker
against Bill Smith

(a faceless
conservative flack
preaching low taxes).

The guy
I'm next to
pipes up:

"Don't people
like that
East Indian guy?

Like, he gets
what Calgarians
seem to be about."

There's a
weird tension
in that.

In the way
Nenshi's set up
as not Calgarian

but also
a positive force
for Calgarians.

But the guy's
legitimately happy
to meet me –

another person
from Alberta
(he's from Edmonton).

A bizarre
race-swapped refraction
of that scene

in Dionne Brand's
A Map to the
Door of No Return

where she
and a friend
find kinship

with the driver
and a
Salish woman

through forms
of relation found
in spatial loss.

Except all
I get
is discomfort

and a desire
to get to
Terminal faster,

fleeing from
the guy's
unwanted friendliness,

though I get
there's no
way to divest

from automatically
beneficial structures
of whiteness.

I'm always
friends with
that guy,

whoever else
he happens
to be.

Long detail. Drunk nerd
insult. Contrary search art. Grocery
firing theatre. "Fake playlist." Struggle
management. "I have a fast-paced
heart." Vintage description waves. "How
can people study these things without
irony?" Conversation redirection notice.
Creamy sauces. App Indigeneity.
"Cormorants are eating fish real hard."
"Storm, car wreck, etc." Linguistic
feedback. Long ago, long ago, etc.

07/20/12

INTO MILLIONAIRING
PARK FRONT

What does
Koolhaas say?

Something about
zoning envelopes?

New York emerged
into its coding

like Chinatown recoded
out of its history?

Something about
density as potential?

Some kindergarten
me-too rule set?

That Starbucks at
Main and Keefer,

designer cocktails
around the corner,

where penthouses
resculpt blocks?

HELL OR HIGH WATER

A civic
optimist's T-shirt.

Resource-rich
bright smiles.

Risk high,
rodeo right.

High River,
high times.

Settlement rhythm's
woke rezoning.

Bank erosion's
happy sandbag.

Boomtown shrugs
its gold rush.

Goldfish tanks
its growth.

A thirsty pitch
after a brand

new headquarters:
"Hey Amazon,

not saying
we'd fight

a bear
for you,

but we
totally would."

Only a
bull market.

Only millions
spent bailing.

BLOCKS AND BLOCKS OF
FOREVER HOUSES

Too much
water imagery?

Maybe more
lines about wind?

Weather too cold
a metaphor

for renovicting
a century-wide lot.

Crisis neighbours
normalize façades.

Prop up fronts
to vacate guts.

Line up cut-outs
to make a block.

A static circularity
unevenly obscures.

No frontier without
frontier heritage.

A glowing *W*
hung in the sky.

Is art a buckling
department store?

A suspension bridge
between bungalows?

Complexity anchors
each owner

to instead support
no foothold.

Souvenir key.
"Tell them about the deal." Smaller
and hotter. "Am I allowed to say
an elder figure?" Prayer sort. Key
to chair. "Not so much a reading
as a rereading." English as cultureless.
"English running-dogs outfit." Crossword
puzzle English. Diction not syntax.
Dictionary readings. Oulipian non-
poetics. Pick and choose. "The too
natural or unnatural." Mastering
language without respect. Ninety-
five. "Mother lose her children to
English." Sardines, not sadness.
Pop song as "a certain kind of prayer."
Family trampoline language. Word
twinning. Where in awareness? Where's
the end? "The scene described
where I was living." Word twinning
melody. Sighs. Working fjord. Horse
and sacrifice. "I'm sure I'll be
eating an egg in my English."

09/29/12

BANFF TRAIL,
LITTLE MOUNTAIN

Are there words
for space that
aren't consumptive?

For digesting
a neighbourhood
swallowed whole?

When viewing
this attractive
gentle grade,

stand in front
of the lobby,
like snowshoeing

but with a chance
to see two small
accounts merge,

intimacy brokered
at multiple
growing scales.

Accelerating pace,
you can't answer
zoning with words

circulated along
Broadway or
Confederation –

"no more comfortable
a place to be
than home" –

street trees,
sidewalk design,
local amenities,

tree-lined bikeways,
all the energy
in these streets,

an echo
of sunlight
and civic cleanliness,

something about
the city's soul
and the plan's clarity.

POODLE PARK,
ST. PATRICK'S ISLAND

Quote unquote
neighbourhood.

Millionairing
parkfront.

Riverfront improv
vacancy magic.

Strip mine conflict,
renovict capacity.

Discourse light-
rail cool.

Food truck
mountainview.

Mayor Moonbeam,
Mayor Sunshine.

Major dad,
Major babe.

But Quarry Park's
no quarry.

Riverbend's no
bent river.

FALSE CREEK, RECONCILIATION BRIDGE

We don't
want to
erase history,

but do
want to
fill in

the gaps we
made draining
the inlet.

What do
the internet
comments say?

Something about
not paving
over the past

like rail yards
packed into
East Van.

How 12th Ave.'s
a fucking
gong show now.

You could drive
through downtown
in four minutes,

but new
spatial practices
disrupt the old.

But this isn't just
a bad analogy,
it's bad planning.

Not happy times
or happy cities,
but a poised eraser.

And no one
agrees to
change history,

but history
does its work
anyway.

That statue
in Charlottesville
inspiring klansmen.

Their car
(our car?)
cuts though crowds.

The bridge
still shapes
the traffic flow

like law and
surveillance
shape cities

from gardens
to trash cans
to prisons

(or playgrounds,
depending on
who's speaking).

But maybe
that's too obvious
for folks

who start
history
in 1492

(except for
the Bering
Land Bridge,

which is
very important
apparently).

New knowledge. Myth,
meme. "In the way the novel was
composed." Advocating rebellious
behaviour. "Heart of gothic darkness."
Reliability unbound. Creature denial.
Domestic affection. "How can I describe
my emotions at this catastrophe?"
Irrational response to rational project.

09/19/12

BUT TO THOSE THAT I LOVE
LIKE A GHOST IN THE FOG

In a bed, weeping.
On script.

Popular whatever.
Half-man, half-mirror.

Reddit spectre.
Expecter.
Inspector.

Move what.

Clinical everything.

Cut teeth.

New grids.

Morsel register.

Order returns order.
Difference sink.

Kitsch Medusa.
Quiet, noun.

Monopoly plastic.
Smack correct.

Mine after mine after mine.

Chaise, change.
Vaseline, vacillate.
Immobile, gauche.

Lock suit.
Luxury box.

Ghost chalet.
Natal gondola.

Decor theory.

In a box, sleeping.
Keepsake nation.

Window cropping.
In shock, in agreement.
Retrograde something.

Fact check.
Jaw checkmark.
Clear table.
Mark clear.

Don't open.

Done up.

Bad concession.

Sum some.

Admit it.

window. Overhead heat. New flow
people. "It's a spotlight." Crusoe
escapes. Our island change. Weather
as the intensity of seeing. Bright
shipwreck. "Art of the young in the
cities." Work father birth. Nation shed.
Brick in Brickhouse. Stoop lamp. Loss
process. Fatal world that is the rock.
A thousand threads. "If one had been
born here, how could one believe it?"
Solution city. Bourbon origin. Celeb
genealogy. Our morning informations.
Levelled custom. Betweened footing.
Coming to the reader's conclusion.
Taming our descriptions. "I slept in
a treehouse last night." Woodlog
castle. BC to Québec. "I feel like
I'm reading poetry all the time." Pipe
filled with gas. Fart breath. Stacked
architectures. "That might be what I
like about sentences." Scaffold plank.
Our Robertsonian precarity. "It is not
called doubt." Foreign fact. Fort
fountain. Pursuit mirror. Unsure gush.
Pin fountain. Archaeological rig. Detail
fear. Feminist categories. "It's not secret
information." Siege sites.

07/14/12

DOES YOUR HOMETOWN CARE?

Did you bring
this weather
with you?

If a body expects
a certain level
of sunlight,

is sunlight
just a metaphor
for friendship?

The water
is still there,
but the waves

desynchronize
against the
shoreline.

What did
Latour mean
in his essay

about songbirds
disrupted by
the freeway?

That the distinctness
of a place
is just relation

tumbling together
or apart
in a pattern

or a logic that
halts other
forms of relation,

working so well
that even Latour
can't recognize

colonialism when
it's described in
his metaphors.

ALL OF OUR WORK IS
BECOMING MORE COMPLEX

Walking down
West Georgia
on the north side.

Across the street,
Telus's window
celebrates Pride

by celebrating
their expansive
LTE network:

"Love is
the greatest
connection."

A block down
another slogan
courtesy of Westbank,

across from
the VPL's
Central branch:

"Culture
reflects
society."

Is this
the best
we can do?

Our relations
and affects
only grist

for the
ongoing millwork
of value generation?

I turn
the corner
at Beatty,

heading to
Anahita's reading
at 8EAST

(an art space
in Chinatown,
formerly Selectors' Records).

They've replaced
the BC
history mural

with something
by a group of
Indigenous artists.

Which is great,
but what happens
to *this* piece

when the
new VAG
goes up

in the
mural-adjacent
parking lot?

Will they
build up
around it

like the
King Edward
Hotel in Calgary?

Now, the fabled
blues venue
only a

"cornerstone
for the development
of the East Village"

folded into
Studio Bell, near
the new library.

HOLD IT TOGETHER NOW

The good
feeling of a
whole movement.

Have we
got enough
sunscreen

to let them
know they're
not welcome?

A routine
that helps
hold things down.

Though tweeting
as transit cops
check fares

is different than
posting Checkstop
locations.

Moving above
grade into
a garden suite,

it's not like
I'm doing
very much,

but at least
I have more
than one room.

Too much space
for a lonely
bachelor

(but not
enough for
his books).

This far from
capitalism there's
easy romance.

Publish another
chapbook away
from the cash.

Develop some
small-press free-
speech algorithm.

One more essay
where poetry
can decolonize

if you don't
count the returning
land part.

One more time
where artists
rent rooms

in emptied
oil towers
downtown.

What could
Oppen do
other than quit?

WET CITY, DRY CITY

Something about
sandcastles swept
into the ocean?

Flooding the
city with
a dense potential?

Planning
with your
fingers crossed?

It's hard to
start from
the middle,

dealing with
the million
flowers

of saying that
the problem is
how things harden.

For fuck's sake,
stop referencing
so much theory.

Sunset loud
against your
cornea.

Days too long
and empty except
for wood smoke.

This city
is hell
in August.

And even trying
to be direct
you can't be.

Title disagreement.
Our absent biographies. Casino
gun drawer. Rust erosion. "The world
is a fucking small place, but the sun
is big." Horse real. Community poetic.
"Contained, gated seniors' community."
Collection status. Echo technique.
Re-entering community. "Complicit in
the secret of the fact, yet nevertheless."
Our relational caution. "Decentralizing
stories, in a way." Red box. Typewritten
heyday. Possibility of cursive abstract.
Between text and divinity. Text-flap
delta. Sense sharpener. Text math.
Psychopath syntax. "Logorhythm and blues."
Broetic quality. Unsprung trap stain.
Being after being. "Wrong object
selection." Information society allusions.
Replacing violent strikes with pain.
Masculine mastery diversion. Our
gendered confidences. A study in
cultural clicks. "A real man accumulating
men." Anxiety of experience. Between
sharing and accumulating. Expert
explicitation.

08/11/12

THE CITY DWELLER IN
PERPETUAL MOVEMENT

What is it
that Lefebvre
argues?

Something about
space not being
a static container?

Doesn't he say
that soon we'll
all be neighbours,

because the whole
world will be
the same city?

One Great Pacific
Garbage Patch
of urbanization.

The rabbits
consume the
campus lawn.

Just dead grass
in the mid-
August heat.

That thin haze
of wildfire
smoke.

Are things
connected or
totalized?

Just let me
turn off Twitter
and see.

HOW MANY CIRCULATING
MATERIAL LOGICS IS THAT NOW?

I mean,
I live here,
but I'm not alone.

A whole set
of real
abstractions,

shaped by
all these
expressive codes.

The bend at
18th under
the poodle

a grown-over
vacant lot
before I moved in.

Something like
the names we use
to describe ourselves

by describing
all these shades
of white.

If I forget
to locate
myself,

this poem
could act
as that pin.

Right now,
at the 49th Parallel
on Main.

Tomorrow,
at the Beano
off 17th.

WHAT DO WE SHARE BUT THE WISH TO SEE RIGHT RELATION?

While the urban
scale spends,
mostly in bed,

imagining
in someone
else's dream,

my landlord
tears out
the shower,

replaces the
water-damaged
drywall.

Any fix
a potential
renoviction.

I'm lucky in
my rent bubble,
though.

My archive
pushed right
into my frame.

"How do you see
the house?" is only
a property question.

Tasks that set
relation right
to ownership.

As in, I own this
bed and laptop
and these books.

URBANIZATION AS METHOD

How did
Haussmann
redesign Paris?

Add a few
lanes for
car traffic,

only to push
them back
for retail.

Don't get
too attached
to models

like the heart
or lungs
or bodily whatever.

I mean,
my everyday
is pretty small.

Tied to the utopia
of not needing
to drive everywhere.

So why run the
Southwest Transitway
along 14th St.

or the SkyTrain
through Kitsilano,
for instance?

Commercial just
narrow enough
to jaywalk,

but 16th
wide enough
to have to run.

I can walk
aimlessly at night
in relative safety

as the cascading
roofs built
in the 1970s

captured in this
book on Calgary
architecture

(bought from
a Vancouver
bookstore)

waterfall into
curlicued wide
streets

like the ones
built during
the last boom.

But cyclists
treat Ontario like
the Tour de France.

The bike share
extends there –
only $129/year,

unlimited half-hours,
but with overage
fees of $6/hour.

THE WORDS TO SAY IT

Something
about bridges
as a metaphor.

The wet feeling
of everything
outside the body.

That's the city
you've been
living in.

Immaterial
labour the bad
bad joke

behind the
"Good Feels
Good" decal.

Spaces made of
those "How are
you doing?" texts

just a question
of cables
under the ocean.

Hey, at least
you have somebody
to talk to

only a
Victorian prescription
for neoliberal times.

UNDER THE CONDOMINIUM SIGNS

Chalked onto
the sidewalk
at Main and 20th

just outside the
Bean Around the World:
"Goodbye Main St."

Melodramatic, sure,
but we all worry
about neighbourhood

after neighbourhood
erupting in a city
after great ones.

The same people
shoved into
the same rooms,

expected to
act genial
or be friends.

A note I left
in Montgomery's
Happy City:

"All examples
based in
capitalist innovation,

moves from
product
to service."

From urban
design to individual
psychology.

From walkability
metrics to let's
grab a coffee.

"Pretend you're listening to a qualified political philosopher." Social affect. Reflecting collectivity. Congealed labour. Our crisis feedback. "Air, water, labour, life." Systemic change as realistic. A study in stark clarity. "A demand for real democracy now, made manifest by the continual presence of people in the streets." Resuscitation sphere. That real alternative. No structures other than structure. Tentative communism. Tented democracy. Our future sharing. "How do we give us our futures back?" New unity. Narrowing the enemy. Our world wants. Historical coax. Class availability. "An old joke from communist times." Red ink, shock prep, etc. More filled participation. Convergence call. Fear past. End poem. "The particulate of the zeitgeist." Social branding. "The symbols of revolution were there to hand." Cat and mouse. "Embedded academic." Reserve army. Low-level danger. Folding everything into everything. Negative consensus. Clearing house.

09/23/12

WHAT CAN I SAY ABOUT IT ANYWAY?

The 20
cutting across

the window's
low vantage

curtains up
kitty-corner,

slow moisture
down concrete.

A block
any direction

invites some
theatrical metaphor.

A stage,
not factory,

not network
or assembly.

"A theatre
of social action."

A dialectic
between choreography

and improv,
I guess.

THE GEOGRAPHY CLOSEST IN

Looking out
the window

just over the
luxury resale

at the tops
of trees

just one
block over.

Main Street's
so tourist heavy

on any
summer Sunday,

but tourists
from Woodbine,

or Marpole,
or wherever.

The tight
shared table –

mixed use in
the worst sense –

my workspace,
your doughnut space.

What do
awkward smiles

code in predictive
urban models?

The three
MacBooks

on this bench
are probably

being used
for work,

though the
Wi-Fi is off

to discourage
camping.

That's not
a metaphor

for anything
other than

the limits
of touch

in our
shared spaces.

NOBODY DOESN'T LIVE
HERE ANYMORE

Again it's
the secondary
suite debate

with its
predictable arguments
about parking,

about renters
as poor,
unattached agents,

posing
a danger
to children

who need
to learn
to be owners.

Vacant lots
need to
meet culture,

at least
that's Westbank's
spicy take

in their
art show
slash advertisement.

"We learned
the price
of everything

yet know
the value
of nothing."

Value constantly
circulates through
my walk

up Main
and back
for groceries

and nothing
seems so
potently valuable.

It means
you've destroyed
the relations

that hold
a space
together.

ONE THAT PROMISES
BREEZY MOBILITY

How many ways
can I barge
into a room –

into somewhere
where I'm present
but uninvited?

On the SkyTrain
passing through
Commercial–Broadway,

Dropbox has
an ad running
to Burnaby

with the slogan
"Let's keep
it flowing.

The world
needs your
creative energy."

Doesn't Whitehead
say that creativity
involves emergence?

If I remember
the dream where
I saw the future,

but only after
I finally finished
Process and Reality,

maybe I'll
get a clear
sense of things.

But even
without enough
material action,

these theoretical
ideas have
material agency too.

Collaboration
one way
or another.

Land value
boosts
creativity –

surplus space
that "provides
conditions"

all while
"generating
dividends."

What culture
reflects
this society?

Whose blues
get sung in
an emptied space?

UPSCALING TO THE GLOBAL

Something in
the slow panning
of server farms

tugs at the
trolley lines turning
Main to Broadway.

But imagine those
tensile lines as
they ribbon,

braiding slack
against the maypole's
warm logistics

into a cry for help
against an array of
drifting eyes.

Two maritime
metaphors diverge
in a wood:

either a
pirate city of
hard-roped yachts,

or this stressed
workbench and its
sandblasted aluminum.

Looking Glass
sings, "Brandy
(You're a Fine Girl)"

as if that's
the sea-bound
romance we need.

Our metaphors only
tie birds to the wing
of an airplane.

Read any newspaper
(maybe just
the *Guardian*)

to find the maps
tracking the movement
of folks to anywhere.

Well, not anywhere,
but where the lines
open up

or rather, where
they can best
bear more load,

like Frost, if he
thought about
distributive agency

and the fact
not everyone
gets to choose.

The high
stakes of storytelling. Refugee system
changes. Biometric identity. "Bogus
is a flashy term." Reverse-order
questioning. Denying author status.
"The institutional will to listen."
Producing favoured narrations. Narrative
favours. "Bodies speak louder than words."
"Bodies without words." Spoken for. Form
stories. Spoken to. Forum stories. "A call
for narrative that is not immaterial."
Empathetic. "Bogus claims." Not encounter,
but biology. "Never fully harmonized."
The empty weight of a limb. Illegible
to the state. Pathogen. Unfaithful
reproduction. Graphic suture. Condition.
Muddy areas. Recording comprehensiveness.
Comprehension. Collaboration or authorship.
Asymmetrical vocal arenas. Bone noise.
Intergenerational return. "A listing of
names." Video transmission as fake neutral.
From tape to body. Story as quantifiable
data. "The named and the unnamed." Space
as irreconcilable. Criss-crossing imperatives.
Reconciliation industry. Haunt. Translating
multiply. "Gaps as a part of collaborative
practice." Kinship words. Display technology.
"The state remains the same."

11/02/12

BAD MAPS

No homeland unturned.

Money, mitochondria, etc.

Some sequel to *Capital*, huh?

Keep looking.

Simple statements.

Street light calm.

Urban rhizomes.

Wry reterritorializations.

Just jokes.

Remembered impunity, etc.

Hammer and sickle, sickle cell, "cell talk," etc.

Something about borders, bodies, etc.

Freeway shortcut, bird song, etc.

Padlock heart.

Neighbourhood expert, expat, etc.

Some body, huh?

Security gates, simulations, etc.

A crowbar busting relation.

Innovation bailing.

Stencil wing.

Pail states.

Diary eye.

Opacity. Any
discernable character. Silence as
boredom. "All stories are love
stories." Torture duration.
Terror analysis. Is "mundane" the
same as "empty"? Treaty end.
Blank space. Self-register. Standstill
dialectics.

07/26/12

LEFT LYING THERE WITH ALL
HIS WOLVES IN HIS THROAT

Who wants
to live in
a performance?

Palm held
gently against
some curtain.

The stupid
optimism of
"Vienna on the Bow"

just the Garden
City transplanted
onto the prairie.

Mawson and Marsh
basically the same
modernist,

except Mawson
didn't knock down
Forest Lawn

(but he would've
if history gave
him the chance).

Why get so
sad over
unbowed strings

that would've
only played
the same tune?

SELF-CRITIQUE IS ALL WE HAVE

Don't get
too sentimental

but don't
abandon sentiment.

Start piling
up books

along the
picture window.

What did
Rich say?

Something about
locating self

inside massive
historical structures?

Something about
the clinamen

rains hard
on the city.

I make friends
with neighbours,

but only
on the PS4.

See what
they're playing.

Maybe *GTA V*
or *Peggle 2*.

Both exercises
in chance,

in pinballing
off algorithms

to shake
them apart.

THERE'S A LIMIT TO YOUR LOVE

And here I
go again,

complaining about
the weather

as if it's
my job.

Like that
one time,

in line at
London Drugs,

the one
on Hastings

just east
of Nanaimo,

breaking into
stark complaint

to the cashier
ringing me up.

Maybe it's
too hot,

but anyway
weather registers

as a near-
universal thing

like money
is universal.

Only weather's
much different

when Christina
Sharpe writes it.

The relational sway
of antiblackness

catching in
the chinook

differently than
Kroetsch's walk

through those
Beltline streets

where getting lost
can break

the city's
oppressive grid

because he's
not being policed.

Pollen tossed
in the wind

another metaphor
for urban life

you can roll
your eyes at.

IT KEEPS CHANGING FAST, IT DOESN'T LAST FOR LONG

Waiting for
the 72
Circle Route,

I chat
with a
local

about the
C-Train extension
into Ogden

and the
expectation of
condo development

like the
pockets around
the SkyTrain,

the resistance
against the viaduct
in Strathcona,

the way
Calgary's roads meet
Vancouver's buildings.

On the 24,
driving past
the site

of the
Shamrock Hotel,
recently demolished,

though they
saved the
hotel's sign,

like the Lido
in Kensington,
the Cecil downtown,

as if texture
were a form
of memory.

All these
ghosts of
relations past

just steam
pouring off
the wastewater

on the 24
heading north
on Ogden Rd.

past the
yeast smell
of the distillery.

It's all
so 1970s,
isn't it?

Or 1990s
or 1950s
or whenever.

Did you
know about
the residential school

where the
Calf Robe
Bridge is now?

Just south
of the
Bonnybrook Plant

on the
north side
of the Bow?

That's where
this article
places it anyway.

I found it
in the VPL's
stacks downtown.

BUT BY THEN IT WOULD
BE WINTER

When Ian Tyson
writes about
Alberta's weather,

he's right, but
Van is great
in the spring.

The array of
kids on laptops
and tablets

along the
angled bench
of this Starbucks,

hard at work
killing time under
a concrete overhang.

What spaces
make them feel
so restless?

Bound by
the good times
of mixed relations

in the social space
of any Calgary
parking lot

squeezed up
into this Marine Dr.
condo complex.

We're all paying
to sit near the
complimentary Wi-Fi,

but also
the exposed
duct work,

feeling warm wind
or smoke over
the mountain,

but the point is
there is no other
side to the mountain.

Always a wager.
An unaccepted premise. Capitalist
time. Our future histories. Making real
the reality of history. "I hope that
we will reach a time that feels
strangely different than the day
before." Our utopian dystopias.
Chronically uneven. Kingpin bishop.
Peculiar mediums. "The delay
between one episode and the next."
City, state, globe. Sitcom flight.
Return fantasies. Both protagonist
and ideal worker. Unrelentingly narrative
dynamic. Spartan fox. Smile
ranking. "Competing for a spot among
the average." Happiness crisis. Our
self-help reversals. "To dream of two
equal forces." Cartoon enlightenment.
Paved complex. Left mountain. Obtained
licence. Property cancels out critique,
making a happy movement. "But through
the body." Personal airspace. A mapped
interiority. Body contest. Our legislation
revolts, dislodging new quarters. World
texts. Semi-peripheral. Midnight forecast.
Even early stages. Uneven modernities.
"Beneath all calculation." "Fetishized with
the fetish." Comforting narrative. Our
labouring interest. "Be careful on whose
behalf you are making a revolution."
Message dissemination. Campaign

principles. Shape issue. Specialized
stupidity. A means of distortion and
torment. "Stupidity becomes a
structural component." Withering tip.
Temporal manifold. Gravitational
independence. "When we are bored,
everything is boring." Objective
mutations in the subject. "Falling
out of frequency with the other."
Counting ceiling tiles. "The situation
could be described as casual."
Olfactory outside. Bodily refuse,
bodily margins. Quotidian mall rat.
Weeping daddies. Our routine secretions.
"In the wake of my odour." Residual
pernition. Crystal myriad. Spectral
waste. Surveillance and administration.
Simple dupe. "Love your destiny."
Ghost ship. Intellectual potentialities.
Reflection and fancy. Glamorous manufacture.
Infinite stacks of boxes. Flowing and
flowing and flowing. "Are we in a
qualitatively different moment?" Gut
feelings. Machines and groomers. Walls
of subsistence. "A step that can't be
taken in various contexts." Our spatial
fixities. Empire in a province in a
city. All that's left is a map of the
ways the poetic is economic. Solitary
player. Several paper towels. Competing
theatres. Apocalyptic symptoms.

"Representations of catastrophe from
the outside." Parts and other parts.
Planes over everything, waves of
fireworks. "The future is a hospital."
New worry. Crisis, then crisis. Nothing
to term. "The end of literature."
Feudalish. Civil brink. Systems
modelling systems. Emergent positive.
Stunted organisms. Freckle fetish.
A sword-point eye. Money fetish. Mere
vivid corporeal life. Sock architecture.
Our zombie pasts. "A broad dimension
of simultaneities." Download fantasy.
Properly endless components. Difference
relates. Between system and agency. Between
human and animal. False new. "Seeing
with a social eye." Dismantling
collectivity. Anti-narrative. Bitmap
cathedral. Species rhetoric. Solid
generation. This so-called trauma.
"Is it too dark?" Doubled apartment.
Image therapy. "It is some time since
they have divided their own
country into squares." Monument
disgrace. "It is nothing else than a
path." Messianic fail. Indices of
absence. Our legible sources. Toilet
gold. Obsessive lengthening. Fragmenting
worker communities. Wage resource.
Distorted acting out. Our elastic days.
Profit moments. "We never get to punch

out." Ripe excess. The profitable fall of
the earth into the sun. Food and
restaurant interiors. Handsome, discrete,
comfortable, nostalgic. Projector fan.
"What is human about humans?" Eyeball
food. Taking up space. "A fantasy of the
agora." Just showing up. Both product
and tool. Over-present entity. Our affective
debts. Cheering for the sheriff. Debt
strike. "This is the real world." Public
sinkholes, social organisms. "A contest
of the disciplines." Allergy demands.
Our governing reticence. Needs
state. "The movement you want is
already underway." Tramp utopia.
Escape from the urban. Temporary
utopian enclaves. "All society becomes
a factory." Occupy nothing. Secular
crisis. Seeds hostile to subjects.
Autumn rents. Nightmare of technicality.
Soil and worker. Our homeless
hierarchies.

06/25/12 – 06/29/12

WHITE

Tally-Ho

Ottertail

Kicking Horse

Amiskwi

Collie

Ensign

Blaeberry

Morrissey

Hartley

Snow Valley

Mere Mortal

Cedar Bowl

Akamina

Snowshoe Trail

Yarrow

Prairie Bluff

South Castle

Grizzly Creek

Lookout

Sunkist Ridge

Carbondale Hill

Mountain Pass

Trailhead

Snowmobile

Summit

Cutline

Maligne

Signal Mountain

Sheep Skin

Goalie

Gorge Water

Lorette

Forgetmenot

Powderface

Station Flat

Sibbald

Stoney Plain

Wapta

Yoho Blow

Skoki

Mosquito Pass

Mistaya

Fossil Dust

Icefield

Pulpit Peak

Lace Falls

Deer Feather

Spray River

NOTES

Coast Mountain Foot refracts the gesture of George Bowering's 1968 collection *Rocky Mountain Foot* – a book where Bowering, upon moving to Calgary for work, proceeds to write (and often complain) about the city for over a hundred pages before ending the sequence with a triumphant return to Vancouver. Rather than return the favour, *Coast Mountain Foot* responds to my own move from Calgary to Vancouver in 2011 by interlacing the connections and conflicts between the two cities. The work here was written in both cities over the span of a decade and a half.

The colonial settlement of Calgary is on Treaty 7 territory, and that territory is the home of the Niitsítapi ᓯᖧᒄᐧᖧ, Tsuut'ina, Stoney Nakoda, and Métis peoples. It's ironic that I needed to move away to reflect on settler colonialism as an organizing fact about the place I was born. I remember the discomforting belatedness I felt as I attended events in Vancouver where Land Acknowledgments were already old hat. I learned over and over (and needed to learn over and over) that the colonial settlement of Vancouver is located on the unceded, Traditional, Ancestral Territories of the xʷməθkʷəy̓əm, Sḵwx̱wú7mesh, and səl̓ilwətaʔɬ peoples. I learned something of the messy and violent realities of land, space, and geography, including the ways they were papered over by the maps I had to memorize and colour in during Social Studies at Sherwood Junior High.

The short-lined lyrics that make up much of the book were written between 2016 and 2018, often during quick breaks from writing my doctoral dissertation on space and poetry in Canada. They came out of an attempt to write poems on my phone while riding the bus and, even though I had to stop writing on transit because of motion sickness, the poems retain a focus on quickness and movement.

"Lord, I'm Set to Cry," "But to Those That I Love like a Ghost in the Fog," and "Bad Maps" were originally drafted while living in a shared house ("The Ranch") in 2005 and 2006 in Calgary and revised in 2017 in Vancouver (living below fellow Calgary expats Chris and Sandy Ewart).

The dated poems come from a notebook kept from May to November 2012, in which I recorded various lectures, talks, seminars, and readings during the first and second years of my Ph.D. at Simon Fraser University. Lines in quotation marks are direct quotes from someone in the room.

The poems throughout the book reference and quote an array of sources that circulated in some way when I was writing:

"Coast Mountain Foot" name drops "Over and Over" off Fleetwood Mac's *Tusk*, heard one morning walking down Main Street from the speakers of Joe's Grill.

"More like Coasting Through" references a post-flood Tourism Calgary YouTube video titled "Calgary, Our Doors Are Open" and John Denver's *Rocky Mountain High.*

"Vancouver Does Not Taste like Calgary" is a riff on a line from a broadside by Mia Rushton and Eric Moschopedis from their *Hunter, Gatherer, Purveyor* project, which hung in the living room of my Vancouver apartment just off Main Street. I read "Luxury never makes anyone beautiful" on the wall of the Abnormal Beauty Company at Hastings and Howe from the window of the Starbucks across the street. This poem was originally published as part of the Spotlight Series (thanks to rob mclennan).

"Yet Another Long Poem about Vancouver" references Daphne Marlatt and Robert Minden's *Steveston* (with apologies to Minden for leaving him out of the poem), Helen Potrebenko's *Taxi,* and Roy Kiyooka's *Pear Tree Pomes.* Amy and Sean are Amy De'Ath and Sean O'Brien. The Paper Hound is a great bookshop on West Pender.

"06/23/12" records the creative event for Friendship as Praxis, the SFU graduate conference, held at the Rhizome Cafe on East Broadway. It featured readings by Nick Beauchesne, Karen Correia Da Silva, Amy De'Ath, Chris Ewart, Jaime Lee Kirtz, Will Owen, and me, and was hosted by Sarah Aplas and Sean O'Brien.

"Lord, I'm Set to Cry" was published in an earlier form as a chapbook by No Press.

"11/13/12" records an event I can't remember.

"It Livens Up a Dead Space" quotes the *Mainlander* article "Vancouver Mural Festival: The Present Is a Gift for Developers" by Jesse Mckee and Amy Nugent and references the slow development of Calgary's East Village over the past decade.

"Just a Quick Snapshot" quotes the Doobie Brothers' "What a Fool Believes" (via the web series *Yacht Rock*).

"Everything I Took I'd Soon Return" takes its title from the Fleet Foxes song "Bedouin Dress" and references Julia Kristeva's *Black Sun*.

"05/28/12" records the week's seminar in David Chariandy's grad class.

"The Economic Case for Tackling Loneliness" quotes L.T. Leif's song "Oh My."

"And Tomorrow, I'm Someone Else" recounts a partial history of Calgary's tallest buildings and references *Wonderland* and *Alberta's Dream* by Jaume Plensa (outside The Bow), the 2013 exhibit *Art for an Oil-Free Coast*, and the statue of George Vancouver on the steps of Vancouver City Hall.

"You Can't Just Take a Name" draws extensively from Taylor Lambert's *Sprawl* article of the same name. The title is a statement made by Siksiká Chief Strater

Crowfoot from a 1993 *Calgary Herald* article about the use of the Crowfoot name in development in northwest Calgary. The first stanza is taken from the snarky lead of a 2015 CBC listicle titled "7 Names for Calgary before It Became Calgary," which side-eyes the fact that the Niitsítapi, Stoney Nakoda, and Tsuut'ina words for the area currently known as Calgary all, in some way, mean "elbow." As we were copy-editing, Charles Simard noted some more names: otōskwanihk ᐅᒍᐣᑲᐧᓂᐠ, meaning "at the elbow," in nēhiyawēwin ᑐ‖ᐃᐧᐁᐧᐃᐧᐃᐧ (the Plains Cree language) and Klincho-tinay-indihay, meaning "town of many horses," in Dene Dháh ᑌᐟ ᒪ (the South Slavey language).

"The Energy in These Streets" references the 2017 city election in Calgary and Dionne Brand's *A Map to the Door of No Return*.

"07/20/12" records an event I can't remember.

"Into Millionairing Parkfront" references Rem Koolhaas's *Delirious New York* and the fight over the development of 105 Keefer Street.

"Hell or High Water" takes its title from T-shirts produced by the Calgary Stampede in the wake of the 2014 flood and quotes from Calgary's 2017 pitch to become the home of Amazon's HQ2.

"Blocks and Blocks of Forever Houses" balances between Vancouver's Woodward's Building and Calgary's Wreck

City, an event in late April 2013 that transformed a row of soon-to-be-demolished houses into a temporary community art project.

"09/29/12" records a reading by jam ismail at KSW's Keefer Street space.

"Banff Trail, Little Mountain" takes its title from two neighbourhoods I've lived in, quotes the promotional language for Paradise Developments' website for Upper Mount Pleasant in Brampton, Ontario, and references the 1941 Congrès international d'architecture moderne's "Athens Charter."

"Poodle Park, St. Patrick's Island" takes its title from two city parks, references two neighbourhoods in southeast Calgary, and name-drops Vancouver's own Gregor "Mayor Moonbeam" Robertson.

"False Creek, Reconciliation Bridge" takes its title from two places that have been renamed. Sen̓áḵw/sən̓aʔqʷ is the name of the area colonially known as False Creek, written in both Sḵwx̱wú7mesh sníchim, the language of the Sḵwx̱wú7mesh people, and in hən̓q̓əmin̓əm̓, the language of the xʷməθkʷəy̓əm people. Thank you to Charles Simard for his expertise and help here (and elsewhere) with Indigenous languages and orthography. Reconciliation Bridge is the new name for the Langevin Bridge, originally named after one of the architects of residential schools and now named after almost nothing. It draws from a thread on the Calgary Reddit page about the development of bike lanes and references the white-supremacist rallies in Charlottesville, Virginia, in the summer of 2017.

"09/19/12" records a lecture from Margaret Linley's first-year undergraduate class. Over the course of the semester, we worked through adaptations of Mary Shelley's *Frankenstein.*

"But to Those That I Love like a Ghost in the Fog" takes its title from Fleetwood Mac's "Angel."

"07/14/12" records "I'm in You, You're in Me" – a "poets presenting poets" talk organized by Louis Cabri at the KSW space on Keefer, featuring readings by Susan Steudel, Marie-Hélène Tessier, Natalie Knight, and Patrick Morrison.

"Does Your Hometown Care?" takes its title from the Superchunk song of the same name and references Bruno Latour's essay "What Is the Style of Matters of Concern?"

"All of Our Work Is Becoming More Complex" takes its title from the copy on a billboard promoting the development at 400 W. Georgia and traces a walk from Pacific Centre to 8EAST before reflecting on the reopening of the King Eddy Hotel as part of the National Music Centre in Calgary ("Studio Bell"). The reading at 8EAST featured a long performance by Anahita Jamali Rad as part of Danielle LaFrance's #postdildo reading series.

"Hold It Together Now" was written after attending an August 2017 rally with Haida Antolick at Vancouver City Hall that was a counter-protest against racist and Islamophobic groups.

"08/11/12" records "I'm in You, You're in Me" – a "poets presenting poets" talk organized by Louis Cabri at the KSW space on Keefer, featuring readings by Amy De'Ath, Emily Fedoruk, and Anahita Jamali Rad.

"The City Dweller in Perpetual Movement" takes its title from a line in Henri Lefebvre's essay "Dissolving City, Planetary Metamorphosis" and references the rabbits that congregate on the University of Calgary campus on summer mornings.

"How Many Circulating Material Logics Is That Now" references Gisele Amantea's untitled public artwork at the corner of Main Street and 18th Avenue.

"What Do We Share but the Wish to See Right Relation?" takes its title from Daphne Marlatt's *Our Lives*. The landlords are Barbara and Richard Cannon. Richard fixed my waterlogged wall pretty quickly.

"Urbanization as Method" references Haussmann's nineteenth-century redesign of Paris, Pierre S. Guimond and Brian R. Sinclair's *Calgary Architecture: The Boom Years, 1972–1982* (bought at the Paper Hound), the controversial bus lanes along 14th Street in southwest Calgary, the equally controversial proposal to extend the SkyTrain into Kitsilano, and the Mobi bike share program.

"The Words to Say It" takes its title from Marie Cardinal's novel of the same name. It references Starbucks's summer 2017 advertising campaign and was written at the Starbucks at Cambie Street and 19th Avenue.

"Under the Condominium Signs" takes its title from Alvvays's song "Forget about Life" and references Charles Montgomery's *Happy City: Transforming Our Lives through Urban Design* (via Calgary city counselor Gian-Carlo Carra's Twitter).

"09/23/12" records an event I can't remember.

"What Can I Say about It Anyway?" quotes Lewis Mumford's essay "What Is a City?" (via Jeff Derksen's first-year course on literature and the city).

"The Geography Closest In" takes its title from Adrienne Rich's "Notes toward a Politics of Location" and was written in the 49th Parallel coffee shop at Main Street and 13th Avenue.

"Nobody Doesn't Live Here Anymore" quotes Claudia Cristovao's manifesto for real-estate developer Westbank's *Fight for Beauty* show and references Calgary city council's never-ending debate over secondary suites.

"One That Promises Breezy Mobility" quotes a slogan for Dropbox and the website for Calgary art space cSPACE King Edward. It references Alfred North Whitehead's *Process and Reality*.

"Upscaling to the Global" references Robert Frost's "The Road Less Taken."

"11/02/12" records a panel talk by Carrie Dawson and Sophie McCall.

"07/26/12" records a Ph.D. cohort meeting led by Marc Acherman.

"Left Lying There with All His Wolves in His Throat" takes its title from a quote in Gilles Deleuze and Félix Guattari's *A Thousand Plateaus* and references both the Mawson Plan (via Kris Demeanor's essay "Ideal City" in Eric Moschopedis and Mia Rushton's *Knock on Any Door*) and the Marsh Plan (via Wayde Compton's *After Canaan* and an excellent paper by Karina Vernon, "Black Canadian Art and the Aesthetics of Spatial Justice," presented at ACCUTE 2016).

"Self-Critique Is All We Have" references Adrienne Rich's "Notes toward a Politics of Location" and Andy Merrifield's *The Politics of the Encounter*. The neighbours (and very real friends) are Chris, Sandy, Hamish, and Finlay Ewart.

"There's a Limit to your Love" takes its title from Feist's song "The Limit to Your Love" and references both Christina Sharpe's *In the Wake* and Robert Kroetsch's "Lines Written in the John Snow House."

"It Keeps Changing Fast, It Doesn't Last for Long" takes its title from John Denver's "Rocky Mountain High" and references two of the major bus routes running out of the Ogden neighbourhood in southeast Calgary. Other than the Vancouver Public Library Central Branch and Strathcona in Vancouver, the locations I mention exist along the 24 Ogden bus route. The article found in the VPL's stacks is "The Short Life of St. Dunstan's Calgary Indian Industrial School, 1896–1907" by Joan Scott-Brown.

"But by Then It Would Be Winter" takes its title from Ian Tyson's "Four Strong Winds" (via Neil Young's cover) and was written at the Starbucks at the Marine Drive SkyTrain station.

"06/25/12 – 06/29/12" records the 2012 Marxist Literary Group conference in Vancouver organized by Carolyn Lesjak and was originally published in *Contours* (thanks to Clint Burnham).

"White" transcribes the names given to shades of white in a General Paint swatch book (thanks to Jason Harbour for giving it to me).

ACKNOWLEDGMENTS

Thanks to all the folks at Talonbooks for publishing one more long poem about Vancouver, even if I made it all about Calgary. Thanks to my substantive editor, Jordan Abel, for offering to print and mail a copy of the manuscript when I said my printer wasn't working and we were in the middle of a pandemic. And thanks to Catriona Strang for her keen copy edits and for hand-wringing with me over the book's sweatier details.

Thanks to Poetry in the Park (organized by Aidan Chafe) and the Strangers on a Train Reading Series (organized by Thor Polukoshko and Heather Jessup) for opening up spaces to perform from this work.

For conversations and camaraderie during the scattered moments of this book, thanks to Haida Antolick, Jonathan Ball, Jason Christie, Steve Collis, Amy De'Ath, Jeff Derksen, Janey Dodd, Mercedes Eng, Chris and Sandy Ewart, Deanna Fong, Joseph Giardini, Christine Kim, Natalie Knight, Danielle LaFrance, Kevin Lee, Laura Leif, Eric Moschopedis, Sean O'Brien, Rajinderpal S. Pal, Julia Polyck-O'Neill, Nikki Reimer, André Rodrigues, Mia Rushton, Andrea Ryer, Nikki Sheppy, Aaron Tucker, Jonathon Wilcke, and you.

And though this book was drafted during my final year in Vancouver, it was revised in Toronto/Tkarón:to during a year where the city I was living in seemed to shrink. Hopefully, this book meets you as our cities open up again!

ryan fitzpatrick

is the author of two previous books of poetry, *Fortified Castles* (Talonbooks, 2014) and *Fake Math* (Snare/Invisible, 2007), and fifteen chapbooks. With Jonathan Ball he edited *Why Poetry Sucks: An Anthology of Humorous Experimental Canadian Poetry* (Insomniac, 2014). He has participated in the literary communities of Calgary, Vancouver, and Toronto. In Calgary, he was on the collective of *filling Station* magazine and was the organizer of the Flywheel Reading Series. In Vancouver, he earned his doctorate at Simon Fraser University, where he worked on contemporary Canadian poetry and space. In Toronto, he recently completed a Postdoctoral Fellowship at the University of Toronto Scarborough and was a co-organizer of the East Loft Salon Series with Rajinderpal S. Pal and Nikki Sheppy.